A Little Life of Jesus

This book belongs to

_____

A Little Life of
Jesus

Retold by Lois Rock

Illustrations by Roger Langton

LION
CHILDREN'S

Text by Lois Rock
Illustrations copyright © 1996 Roger Langton
This edition copyright © 2015 Lion Hudson

The right of Roger Langton to be identified as the illustrator
of this work has been asserted by him in accordance with the
Copyright, Designs and Patents Act 1988.

Published by Lion Children's Books
an imprint of
Lion Hudson plc
Wilkinson House, Jordan Hill Road,
Oxford OX2 8DR, England
www.lionhudson.com/lionchildrens

ISBN 978 0 7459 6567 3

First UK edition 1997
This edition 2015

A catalogue record for this book is available from the
British Library

Printed and bound in Singapore, October 2014, LH02

About This Book

Here is a book about a very special person:
Jesus.

He was born many long years ago, but
people have never forgotten him. His friends
wanted to tell everyone in the world all about
him: the things he did and the things he said.
They wanted everyone to love Jesus as much
as they did.

Some people wrote those stories down:
Matthew, Mark, Luke and John each wrote
their book of stories about Jesus. You can
find their books in the Bible.

Those books are quite long. So, to help
you begin to know all about Jesus, I have
chosen to tell you just twelve stories. I used
the books by Matthew, Mark, Luke and
John to help me.

About the prayers

Jesus said that he was born to show people what God is like. Many people say that the stories of Jesus help them know more about God. Then they want to talk to God: they want to say a prayer. In this book I have put prayers that I wanted to say to God when I had finished writing the story. You can say my prayer to God if you like. You might want to say your own prayer.

The Author

List of stories

Jesus Is Born   page 11
Luke 2:1-38

A story about the baby Jesus, and the people and angels who thought he was so very special.

Jesus Grows Up   page 39
Matthew 2:19-4:21

A story about Jesus' life, from the time he was a little boy to the time he began to tell people all about God.

Jesus' Important Message   page 67
Matthew 5 and 6

Come and listen with the children who gathered around Jesus. Find out what he said about the good and right way to live.

Jesus' Special Prayer   page 95
Matthew 6 and 7

Jesus' friends asked him to tell them how to pray to God. He gave them a prayer to say. All the people who have learned to love Jesus think this prayer is a special one.

If you have ever had to wait a long, long time for someone to come and meet you, then you will understand why people are happy when they hear the news that . . .

Jesus Is Born

Two thousand years ago, the Jews who lived in Israel were sad. Long ago, God had promised to take care of them.

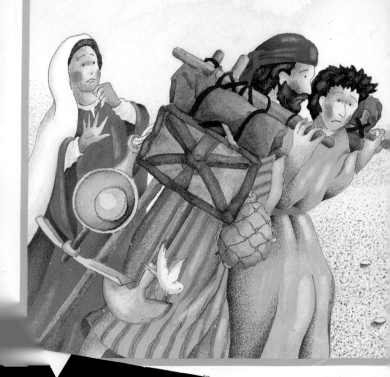

But for hundreds of years, their enemies had beaten them. Right now, it was the Romans who ruled the land.

They looked in the special books that told them the long story of their people.

There, they read that God had promised to send a King to help them. But they had been waiting a long time.

Mary was a young woman who lived in a village called Nazareth. One day, an angel came to talk to her.

"God has chosen you to be the mother of a special baby," said the angel. "You must call him Jesus. He will be God's special king."

Mary told her cousin Elizabeth. "You must be the happiest woman ever," said Elizabeth.

Mary told God how she felt: "Thank you, God, for choosing an ordinary person like me. Thank you for keeping your promise to our people."

But the Romans still ruled the land, and the emperor wanted a list of everyone who lived there.

Mary had to go with Joseph, the man she was planning to marry, to put her name on the list. Together, they went to Joseph's home town of Bethlehem.

Bethlehem was crowded with travellers!
All the rooms in the town kept for
visitors were taken.

Mary and Joseph had to make do with
a room kept for animals to shelter in!

And there, Jesus was born.

Mary wrapped her baby warmly. She had no cradle—but the manger the animals ate from made a safe place to put Jesus.

Shepherds were out on the hills, keeping their sheep safe. Suddenly, an angel appeared... and they were terrified.

"Don't be afraid," said the angel. "Here's good news. God's special king has been born. He's in Bethlehem now. You'll find him lying in a manger."

Hundreds of angels joined in singing!

29

The shepherds went up to the town. They found the baby, just as the angels had said.

A few weeks later, Mary and Joseph went to the temple in Jerusalem—the big city nearby.

They wanted to thank God for the baby.
An old man named Simeon was there.

He held the child in his arms. "Thank you, God, for this baby," he said. "I'll die happy now.

"You have kept your promise: this is your king, who has come to help your people and to show the whole world how great you are."

A Christian prayer

Dear God,
When I feel lost and alone
I will think of the people long ago
who felt lost and alone
and who were glad
that Jesus came to help them.
Amen.

If you have ever been busy,
and then stopped to do
something more important,
then you will understand what
happens when . . .

Jesus Grows Up

Mary was Jesus' mother. An angel had said that her son was God's special King. Mary took good care of Jesus.

Her husband, Joseph, made a home for
them in Nazareth.

41

Joseph was a builder and carpenter. As Jesus grew up, Joseph showed him how to work with wood and stone.

43

As he grew up, everybody in the town knew Jesus as the local builder and carpenter.

Jesus' cousin John did something far more exciting. He lived in the desert, but crowds came to hear what he had to say about God.

"Give up your bad ways and live as God wants," John said to them.

47

If anyone wanted to make a new start,
John baptized them.

He dipped them in the River Jordan as they said goodbye to their old ways...

And lifted them up to show they were making a new start.

One day, Jesus came and asked to be baptized.

"But you don't need it," said John. "Compared to you, it's me who needs to make a new start for God."

Jesus said he must. And as Jesus came up out of the water, God's voice said, "You are my son. I am pleased with you."

Jesus knew it was time for a change. He had other work to do now. But he spent days thinking about it, wondering if he had made the right choice. In some ways, he'd rather be rich, or famous, or important...

But no: he must do as his father God wanted. He must go and tell people about God, and about how to be God's friends.

Down by the lake called Galilee, he saw some fishermen mending their nets.

"Come and help me," he said. "You know what it's like to catch a net full of fish. I need you to help me gather up crowds and crowds of people.

"Because God wants sick people to be made well. God wants sad people to be happy. God wants to welcome people as friends. I'll show you how...

And the fishermen left their nets, and went with Jesus.

A Christian prayer

Dear God,
It's easy to be busy
and hardly think of you.
But you call us
to be your friends,
to do the things you want done.
And that is the most important thing of
all.
Amen.

If you have ever been worried, and wished you weren't a worrier, then you will understand . . .

Jesus' Important Message

Jesus had grown up to become a builder and carpenter. But now he spent his time telling people about God.

Grown-ups jostled to talk to him, to ask him important questions. Some of them were rich and clever, with important jobs.

But Jesus wanted everyone to hear what he had to say.

Everyone was important. It didn't matter
if they were rich or poor.

And whenever the crowds sat down to listen to him, Jesus always had a special welcome for the children.

What he said often sounded simple. But it made people think about important things.

"Imagine that one person tells you to go this way, and another tells you to go that way. Can you obey both of them?

"No, of course you can't.

"Lots of people spend their lives going one way: the way of worrying about money and all the things it can buy.

"I tell you now, that won't make them happy for very long.

77

"Look at the birds flying around. They don't sow seeds. They don't gather crops. They don't store food in barns.

"But God takes care of them.

"Look at the wild flowers. They don't spin thread. They don't weave cloth. They don't stitch clothes.

"But no one has ever had clothes as beautiful as the petals they wear. God takes care of the flowers.

"I promise you this: God is like the kindest parent ever.

"God really loves you. God will take care of you.

"Who is really happy?

"The people who love the God who loves them, and who set their heart on going the way God wants.

"Who is really happy?

"The people who are kind to others, who forgive their enemies, who settle quarrels.

"Who is really happy?

"The people who follow me and live as God wants. Sometimes they are teased and bullied and hurt for being my friends. But they don't give up.

"At the end of time, God will welcome them, and they will be safe and happy with God for ever."

A Christian prayer

Dear God,
You show us the way
we should go.
You take care of us
whatever happens.
Help me to learn to
give up worrying
and put my trust in you.
Amen.

If you have ever been stuck
for what to say to someone
important, you will see why
people asked for . . .

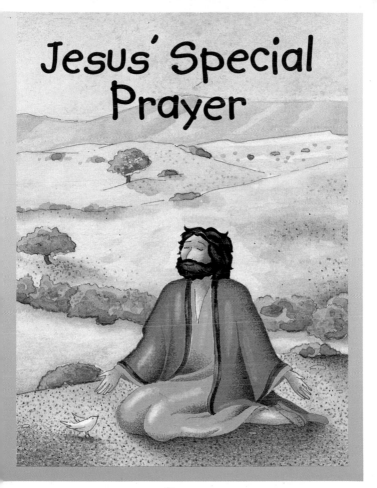

Jesus' Special Prayer

Jesus always welcomed people who wanted to see him.

He always seemed to have time for them.

Jesus always spent time with God, too. Sometimes he got up early and went for a walk in the hills by himself.

There he talked to God and listened to God: Jesus spent time praying.

Sometimes when he wanted to pray, he stayed in a room, quietly, by himself, with the door closed.

"Some people like to pray in a place where everyone will see them," Jesus told his friends. "They are happy just because other people notice how much they pray.

"But you must go somewhere where no one will notice you. Pray to God just as you talk to a father who really loves you. God will hear your prayers."

"What shall we say in our prayers?" asked Jesus' friends.

106

"A short prayer is fine," said Jesus. "God knows what you really want to say anyway. So, pray like this:

"Dear Father God you are greater than anything in this world. You are everything that is good and right.

"I want everyone in the world to know how great you are, so they will treat you as their king and live as you want.

"Please give us the things we need for living today.

"Forgive us the wrong things we have done, as we forgive other people who have done wrong things to us.

"Please keep us safe from anything that makes us want to forget you and disobey you, and from anything that stops us being your friends."

Then Jesus went on to say this to the people listening: "Ask: God will give. Look for God: you will find God. Knock: God will open the door to you.

"God wants to give you good things, and to come and live as your friend always."

A Christian prayer

Our Father in heaven,
hallowed be your name,
your Kingdom come,
your will be done,
on earth as in heaven.
Give us today our daily bread.
Forgive us our sins
as we forgive those who sin against us.
Lead us not into temptation
but deliver us from evil.

For the Kingdom, the power, and the
glory are yours now and for ever.
Amen.

Sometimes a job seems so big and you seem so little. But a little goes a long way when . . .

Jesus Shares a Picnic

Crowds followed Jesus wherever he went. One day, he wanted to be alone for a while.

Jesus and his close friends got into a boat and sailed across Lake Galilee.

But the crowds came hurrying down to the shore on the other side of the lake.

Some were sick: they wanted to be healed. Some had questions about God: they wanted to hear what Jesus had to say.

Jesus welcomed them.

He let the people stay all day—until the sun was beginning to set.

But by now they were hungry. What would it cost to feed all those people? Lots and lots and lots.

Jesus' close friends were worried. They didn't have that kind of money.

Did they have anything to offer? "Well yes," said one of Jesus' friends—a man named Andrew.

"A boy here has five loaves of flat barley bread and two fish."

A picnic for one.

And five thousand hungry people.

"Tell the people to sit down," said Jesus.

So everyone sat down on the grass.

Jesus took the bread. "Thank you, God, for this bread," he said.

And he handed it out to the people close by.

Then he took the fish. "Thank you, God, for these fish," he said.

And he handed those out too.

People took the food from the person next to them.

They broke off a bit for themselves, and passed the rest on.

And on. And on. And on.

Everyone had as much as they wanted.

When the eating was over, Jesus asked his friends to gather up the scraps.

The leftovers filled twelve baskets.

A Christian prayer

Dear God,
You notice little children.
You notice what they have
and what they can do.
Please use the things I have
and the things I can do—and do
wonderful things with them!
Amen.

If you have ever cried
because you have had to
say goodbye to someone you
loved, then you will be cheered
by the story of how . . .

Jesus Heals a Little Girl

One sad day, a father named Jairus sat and worried. His little girl was dying.

Then he heard exciting news: Jesus had just arrived by boat on the lakeshore.

Jesus had made lots of people well.
Perhaps Jesus could help?

The crowd was huge, but Jairus made his way to the front. There, he threw himself down in front of Jesus.

"My little girl is very ill," he said. "Please come and make her well."

156

Jesus agreed to go with him. But how slowly they moved!

The crowds pushed close to Jesus on all sides.

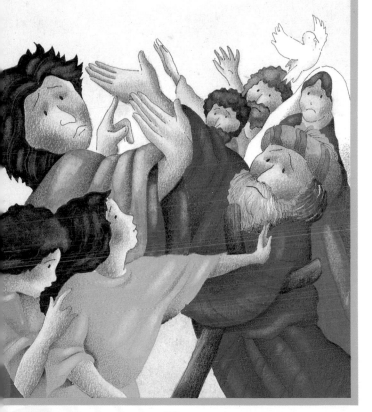

And Jesus seemed in no hurry. He even stopped to talk to another sick person on the way.

Jairus was going frantic with worry.

Then a message came from his home.

"It's too late," people said. "Your little girl has died. There's no point bothering Jesus now."

Jesus took no notice. "Don't be afraid," he said to Jairus. "Go on believing I can help."

He chose just three friends—Peter, James and John—to go on with them.

What a sight there was when they reached Jairus' house! People were weeping and wailing.

"There's no need to carry on like this," said Jesus. "The child is not dead. She's only sleeping."

"What a foolish thing to say," said one woman.

"We've seen her. We know she's dead,"
said another.

"Anyone who has come here to get a funeral ready can go," said Jesus. "There isn't going to be a funeral."

Jesus and his three friends went with the mother and the father to the girl's bed. Her body was very, very still.

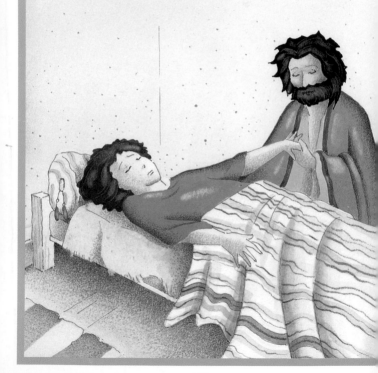

"Little girl," he said. "I'm telling you to get up."

And the little girl got up: ready for a meal, and ready for life!

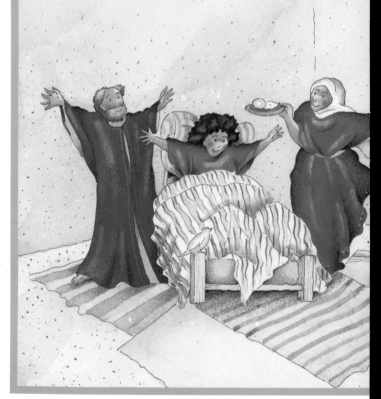

A Christian prayer

Dear God,
Sometimes things seem so bad
it's hard to believe you can help.
But you are stronger
than all the things that make us sad.
Help us to trust in you,
to stay close to you,
and wait for you
to make us glad again.
Amen.

If you have been left out
because you've been
mean, then you will understand
the story of . . .

Jesus and the Man who was Rescued

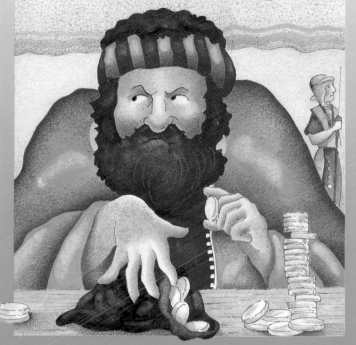

Long ago, in a town called Jericho, lived a man named Zaccheus.

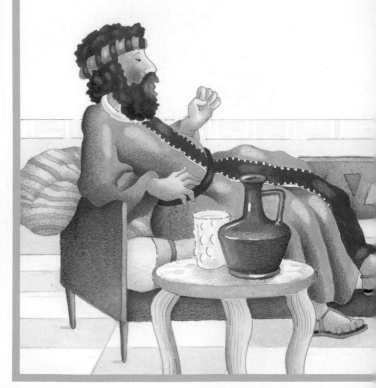

He was very, very rich.

But no one liked him. No one wanted to talk to him. No one wanted to go to his house.

182

Poor Zaccheus! Why didn't he have any friends?

Was it something to do with his job?
Zaccheus was a tax collector. He
collected money from people and gave it
to the Romans who ruled the land.

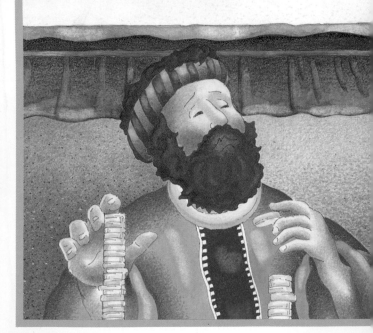

And the Romans told him to collect a little extra for his own wages.

Everyone knew that Zaccheus collected a lot more than he needed to give the Romans.

He kept lots and lots of money for himself.

One day, Jesus came to Jericho. Jesus! The man who could make sick people well; the man everyone wanted to hear.

Lots of people wanted to see him.

Zaccheus wanted to see Jesus too. But he was short.

There were so many people in front of him, that he could not see anything.

So he did a clever thing. He ran ahead, and climbed a tree. Now he could see what was going on. And Jesus was coming that way.

Jesus came to the tree, and stopped. He looked up and said, "Hurry down, Zaccheus. I must stay in your house today." Zaccheus came down very fast. He was so happy! Someone wanted to visit him at last.

Lots of the other people there were angry.

"It's not fair," they grumbled. "Jesus is going to the house of a cheat—the man who makes himself rich and leaves us poor."

Zaccheus and Jesus had a meal together. And they talked.

Something in what Jesus said and did
made Zaccheus want to change his ways.

He stood up and said to Jesus, "Listen. I will give half of all I have to the poor.

"If I have cheated anyone, I will pay them back four times as much."

Jesus was happy. "My work is to rescue people who have lost their way in life," he said.

"And today, someone in this house has been rescued."

A Christian prayer

Dear God,
I am sad when people are mean to me.
I am sad when I am mean.
Please be a friend to mean people.
Show them your love,
and help them to be loving.
Amen.

If you have ever tried to make things perfect and got in a panic *because* it was all too hard, then you *will* be happy to read about . . .

Jesus and the Very Busy Sister

Mary and Martha were two sisters.
They lived in a little house in a village.

One day, Jesus and his friends came to visit.

The two sisters were very pleased. They wanted to do their best to welcome Jesus.

"There are so many things I must do,"
said Martha to herself.

"Jesus will be hot and dusty from walking here. I'll bring water so he can wash.

214

"And I'll make this corner of the room comfortable for him to sit and talk to all the people who want to see him.

"We've got lots to offer to drink...

"and I'll make a big pot of soup and bake extra bread...

"Oh dear, will the fire ever burn and make the stove good and hot?"

Martha got in a panic at all she had to do. And then she saw her sister Mary: just sitting, just listening to Jesus.

Martha felt very cross indeed.

She marched over.

"Don't you care that my sister has left me to do all the work by myself?" she stormed at Jesus. "Tell her to come and help me."

"Martha," said Jesus. His voice was kind. "Dear Martha. You are worrying about so many things. But only one thing is needed. And Mary is already doing it.

227

"I've come to spend time with you, to tell you stories about God and help you understand how much God loves you. Come and listen to what I have to say.

"I'm not going to stop anyone who wants to listen to me. That's the very best thing to do."

A Christian prayer

Dear God,
If you only loved me
because of the busy things I do,
I'd have to be busy all the time.
But you love me because I'm me.
And you want me to sit
and listen to you.
Amen.

If you have ever felt very lost and very small, then you will understand . . .

Jesus' Story of the Lost Sheep

Lots of people liked Jesus. He was always so pleased to see them.

He made people feel special—whoever they were, whatever they had done.

Other people were cross. "You can't be a good person if you talk to people who do bad things," they grumbled. "You can't be very important if you have time for unimportant people."

So Jesus told them this story.

"Imagine," he said, "that you have a hundred sheep. They are out on the hillside, nibbling at plants. You are watching them. 'Are they all there?' you ask yourself. And so you count them.

"There are only ninety-nine!

"You count again. There are still only ninety-nine. You know there are a hundred sheep in your flock. And there are ninety-nine on the hillside. What does that mean?

"It means that one sheep is missing. And you are going to have to do something about it.

"You check that the ninety-nine are still safely nibbling at plants. You take your stick, and off you go, to look for the one that is missing.

"You walk and walk. You peer into thorn bushes. You clamber among fallen rocks. You slither down slopes... Everywhere you go you are anxiously looking and listening.

"And then, at last, you see your missing sheep. Hooray!

"It doesn't matter any more that your feet are hurting. It doesn't matter that you're tired and thirsty. What's important is that you have found the sheep you had lost.

"And gently you pick it up. Gently you put it on your shoulder. Gently you carry it home.

"On the way, you pass some friends. 'This sheep went missing,' you say. 'But I found it. Let's have a party when the flock are all back in the sheepfold for the night.'

"God is like that good shepherd," said Jesus. "God really cares about any person who feels lost. It doesn't matter what they have done. Everyone is important. God wants to find them and be their friend."

A Christian prayer

Dear God,
Sometimes I feel very small
and very alone.
Please come and find me,
and be my friend.
Amen.

If you have ever needed help and been surprised at who bothered to stop, then you will understand . . .

Jesus' Story of
the Kind Enemy

Jesus spent a lot of time telling people about God and listening to their questions.

Some people tried to ask him the hardest questions they could think of. They hoped Jesus would give a wrong answer and end up looking silly.

"What must I do so that I can live as God's friend for ever?" asked one man.

His job was to teach people about God, so he thought he knew the right answer.

"You've read the books with God's laws in," said Jesus. "What do they say?"

The man answered: "First of all, love God. Next, love other people. Be as kind to them as you are to yourself."

"Quite right," said Jesus. "You knew already."

"But which other people do I need to love?" asked the man. So Jesus told this story.

"One day, a man was going down the road from Jerusalem to Jericho. Robbers attacked him and took all he had.

"They beat him up and left him lying hurt in the road.

"A priest came by—a priest from the temple in Jerusalem. He helped people follow God's laws.

"But when he saw the man lying in the road, he pretended not to see and hurried by.

"A Levite came by—a helper in the same temple where people came to worship God.

"He saw the man and came closer to look. Then he hurried away too.

"A Samaritan was also travelling along that road."

Now, people from Jerusalem didn't like Samaritans. Samaritans didn't worship God in the right way and they didn't have a proper temple. Samaritans were enemies to the people listening to Jesus' story.

"The Samaritan saw the man, and he wanted to help. So he bandaged up the man's wounds. He helped the man on to his own donkey and took him to an inn.

" 'Please look after this man for me,' he asked the innkeeper. 'Here are coins to pay for what you do. If it costs more, I'll pay you on my way back.'

"That's the story," said Jesus. "Here's a question. Who do you think showed love to the person who got hurt?"

"The one who was kind to him," said the man.

"Quite right," said Jesus. "Now you go and do the same."

A Christian prayer

Dear God,
Because you love us
we can love you
and we can love ourselves.
Your kindness and love help us learn how
to love others:
to be gentle with our friends,
to be kind to our enemies.
Amen.

If you know what it is like when friends run away and one person is left alone and in trouble, then you will be astonished to read about . . .

Jesus All Alone

It was a day in spring, long ago. Lots of people were travelling to Jerusalem for a special festival.

When they heard that Jesus was coming too, there was great excitement.

294

"I'm going to wave!"
"Let's make a carpet for his donkey to walk on—like they do for kings."

"I've spoken to him," some said. "He was kind to me. He made me feel special. He's my best friend."

At that moment, it seemed that
everyone in the world wanted to be
friends with Jesus. There were smiling
crowds all around.

But Jesus had always had enemies. Some people didn't like the way he talked about God: he said God welcomed people. What nonsense!

"God doesn't want bad people as friends!" they argued. "God wants people who keep the rules. We know the rules. We teach the rules." They wanted to get rid of Jesus.

It was one of Jesus' close friends who let him down: Judas Iscariot.

Judas told Jesus' enemies where they could find him.

That evening, Jesus went to an olive grove to pray. Eleven of his close friends were with him.

Then there was a clatter: Judas led some armed men to take Jesus to his enemies.

Jesus did not try to run. He did not try to fight.

But he must have felt sad when his friends ran away, afraid.

Jesus was dragged before his enemies. They tried to prove he had done wrong things. They told lies about him to get him into trouble.

Jesus didn't argue or shout back.

The soldiers who were told to guard Jesus were used to bullying their prisoners.

They teased him and hit him. Jesus didn't get angry.

The ruler of the country, Pontius Pilate, could see that Jesus had done no wrong. "I always set a prisoner free at the time of this special festival," he said to himself. "I'll ask the crowds if they want me to set Jesus free."

But Jesus' enemies had told the crowds what to say: "Kill him! Crucify him!"

Jesus was all alone. None of his friends dared come near. They were too scared.

Jesus let it happen: all the bad things, all the cruel things, all the unkind things. His enemies put him to death. They nailed him to a cross of wood.

Before he died, Jesus said a prayer to God:

"Father, forgive them. They don't know what they are doing." Jesus loved everyone to the very end.

A Christian prayer

Dear God,
You sent Jesus to show us
how much you love people.
He forgave the friends who ran away.
He forgave the people who hurt him.
Thank you for your love.
Thank you for your forgiveness.
Amen.

If you have ever made a mess of things and wished for a new start then perhaps you will understand . . .

Jesus and the New Beginning

Jesus' friends were sad. Jesus had been killed by his enemies.

They didn't know what to do. So they just wept.

A rich man named Joseph took charge.
"Let me take the body of Jesus," he
said. "I'll bury it."

He and another of Jesus' friends took the body and laid it in a tomb rather like a cave. It had a big round stone that could be rolled in place as a door.

At sunset the weekly day of rest began.
Jesus' friends had to stop what they
were doing.

"We'll go back after the day of rest and wrap the body properly," they said. "That will really be the last goodbye."

When that day came, the women got up very early. They went to the tomb. The stone door had been rolled away!

The tomb was empty. Where was Jesus' body?

Suddenly two people in bright shining clothes stood by them. "Why are you looking in a tomb for someone who is alive?" asked the shining people.

"Jesus is not here. God has given him new life."

The women were amazed. They went back to the others to tell their story.

"That's a silly story," they sneered. "How dare you make up a story like that when we're all so sad?"

But some of them went to check. The tomb was empty. One of the women, Mary, stayed there looking at it.

"I shall ask that man over there to tell me what happened," she said to herself. "I think he's the gardener. Perhaps he came here early."

When she spoke to him, he turned to look at her. "Mary," he said.

And she knew it was Jesus. He told her to go and tell people: he really was alive!

Some time after, other friends of Jesus saw him too. They had gone fishing one night, and when they came back to shore, Jesus was there to welcome them.

He was still their friend. They had fish for breakfast together!

Jesus had a special message for his friends: "Soon, I will go to be with God," he told them.

"You must go and tell everyone the good news about me."

And so they did. They spread the news that God loves people, just as Jesus loved people.

The news that God forgives people, just as Jesus forgave people. The news that God will give a new beginning to anyone who follows Jesus.

And the message goes on and on. It's been spreading for two thousand years. People still hear it and become friends and followers of Jesus.

They believe that one day Jesus will come back and all his friends will live with him: friends with God for ever and ever.

A Christian prayer

Dear God,
When I get things in a mess,
it's so good to know you love me.
Please give me a new beginning
and let me be your friend for ever.
Amen.

Special words in this book

angel
A messenger from God. No one really knows what angels are or what they look like. In the stories of Jesus, it seems that angels look like people, but they are bright and shining—and a bit frightening.

baptize
Dip in water and lift up again. Being baptized is a sign of making a new start.

Bethlehem
A little hilltop town in Israel. It is quite near the big city of Jerusalem. One of Israel's greatest kings was born in Bethlehem. His name was David.

carpenter
A person who works with wood. Jesus learned to be a carpenter.

crucify
Nail someone to a cross of wood to kill them. This was a cruel punishment the Romans had for people

who had broken their laws. Jesus was crucified
because people told lies about him—he hadn't done
the wrong things they said.

Elizabeth
The cousin of Mary, the mother of Jesus. Her son was
John, the one who baptized people.

emperor
The person who ruled the Roman empire. Israel was
part of the Roman empire.

festival
A special celebration. The Jews had festivals to
celebrate the good things they believed God had done
for them.

fisherman
A person who catches fish for a living. Some of Jesus'
best friends were fishermen. They went fishing in little
boats on Lake Galilee.

funeral
A ceremony to say a last goodbye to the body of
someone who has died, before putting it in a tomb.

Galilee
Part of the land of Israel. It has a big lake, Lake Galilee, and hills all around.

God
A name for the one whom the Jews believed was the great maker of all the world. The Jews believed that God had always looked after them, and wanted them to show all the world how good and great is God.

Israel
One of the names for the land where Jesus lived.

Jairus
The name of the man whose daughter needed to be healed by Jesus.

James and John
Two brothers, who were close friends of Jesus.

Jericho
A large town in the land of Israel. It was built around an oasis—springs of water in a hot, dry place.

Jerusalem
The capital city of the land of Israel.

Jews

A name for the people of Israel. Jesus was a Jew.

John

the name of Jesus' cousin. He baptized people.

Jordan

the name of the river that runs through the land of Israel. It flows out of Lake Galilee, down past Jericho and into a big lake called the Dead Sea.

Joseph

The man who married Mary, the mother of Jesus. He worked as a carpenter.

Joseph of Arimathea

A rich man who was sad Jesus had been crucified. He asked for Jesus' body so he could put it in a proper tomb.

Judas Iscariot

One of Jesus' close friends, the one who let him down and told the people who hated him where they could come and catch him.

law

Rules about what to do. The Jews believed God had given them laws about what was right and what was wrong.

Levite

A special name for a person who helped in God's temple in Jerusalem.

Martha and Mary

Two sisters who were friends of Jesus.

Mary

The name of Jesus' mother. She married a carpenter named Joseph. They lived in a town called Nazareth.

Mary

The name of the woman who saw Jesus in the garden by the tomb after he came alive. She came from a village called Magdala, and is often known as Mary Magdalene.

Nazareth

A town among the hills of Galilee, the place where Jesus grew up.

Peter
One of Jesus' best friends.

Pontius Pilate
The name of the Roman who ruled the land of Israel when Jesus was a man. He was in charge of making sure everyone kept the laws made by the emperor.

prayer
Talking to God. A prayer can be something a person says aloud or thinks inside their head.

priest
A person who helps people find out about God. Priests were in charge of the ceremonies at the Jewish temple.

Romans
The nation that ruled Israel and many other countries. Roman soldiers helped make sure that people obeyed Roman laws.

Samaritan
A person from Samaria. This was a region in between Galilee and Jerusalem. People from Jerusalem didn't like Samaritans.

shepherd
A person who looks after a flock of sheep.

Simeon
The name of an old man who spent a lot of time in the temple in Jerusalem praying to God. Mary and Joseph showed him the baby Jesus.

temple
A special building where people go to remember God. They may say prayers or hold special ceremonies to help them remember important things about God. The special Jewish temple was in Jerusalem.

tomb
A place where a dead body is buried.

Zaccheus
A rich man who lived in Jericho. He collected money from the people to give the Romans—he collected taxes.